GO TURBO

ROBOT WORLD

TONY HYLAND

EDGE
FRANKLIN WATTS

LONDON·SYDNEY

First published in 2009 by
Franklin Watts
338 Euston Road
London NW1 3BH

Franklin Watts Australia
Level 17/207 Kent Street
Sydney NSW 2000

Series editor: Adrian Cole
Art director: Jonathan Hair
Design: Blue Paw Design
Picture research: Sophie Hartley
Consultants: Fiona M. Collins and Philippa Hunt,
Roehampton University

A CIP catalogue record for this book is available from the British Library.

ISBN: 978 0 7496 8662 8

Dewey Classification: 629.8

Acknowledgements:
The Publisher acknowledges all © names shown within this title as the property of their respective owners.
Photo courtesy Carnegie Mellon Tartan Racing: 33. Photo courtesy Ecole Polytechnique Fédérale de Lausanne (EPFL): 3 & 41b. Photos by
ECT: 10. ESA/NASA/JPL/University of Arizona: 35 (inset). Photo courtesy FANUC Robotics UK: 9. Robyn Beck/AFP/Getty Images: 22 &
23. David Hecker/AFP/Getty Images: 41t. Toshifumi Kitamura/AFP/Getty Images: 11. © Honda Motor Co., Ltd.: Cover, 19t & 40. Photo
courtesy iRobot: 6, 7t, 14-15, 17, 18t & b, 30t & b, 31 & 32. © iStockphoto.com/Gabor Izso: Endpapers. © iStockphoto.com/Ricardo
Azoury: 8. Image courtesy of the LEGO Group. ® 2009 The LEGO Group: 16, 20. NASA/Ames Research Center: 37. NASA/Jet
Propulsion Laboratory: 34-35, 38 & 39. NASA/Johnson Space Center: 36. Image courtesy NOAA: 12t & b. Sipa Press/Rex Features: 21.
James King-Holmes/Science Photo Library: 19b. © Shutterstock.com/Shawn Hine: 24. Photo courtesy Toyota (GB) PLC: 7b. Photo courtesy
University of Washington: 13t & b. U.S. Air Force photo: 15b

Every attempt has been made to clear copyright. Should there be any
inadvertent omission please apply to the publisher for rectification.

Printed in China

Franklin Watts is a division of Hachette Children's Books,
an Hachette UK company.
www.hachette.co.uk

*Every effort has been made by the Publishers to ensure that the websites
in this book contain no inappropriate or offensive material. However,
because of the nature of the Internet, it is impossible to guarantee that the
contents of these sites will not be altered. We strongly advise that Internet
access is supervised by a responsible adult.*

Contents

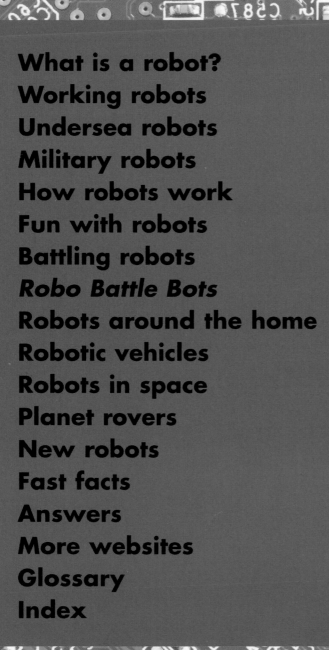

Words that are highlighted can be found in the glossary.

What is a robot?

Robots are machines that can work without a human controlling them. They do not have a brain. Instead, they use computer power to work.

Some machines are called robots, but they are **Remotely** Operated Vehicles (ROVs). Human operators control them. The ROV above is making a bomb safe.

There are many types of robot. Most work in factories and are large machines with just one arm. Other robots move around. Some can fly or even travel underwater.

A lawnmower robot has wheels.

Some robots look like human beings. They are called humanoid robots.

? Look back at the contents page – what do you think will be your favourite type of robot?

Working robots

Most robots work in car factories. Robots are very good at doing the same simple job again and again. Each robot has just one job to do.

A line of robots puts the parts of the car body together. Another line of robots spray-paints each car body.

Today there are over one million robots, such as the welder below, working in factories in Japan, Europe and the USA.

FANUC Robot
ARC Mate 100iC

Arm

Elbow

Welder

Robots can do many other jobs in factories. Some pack things into boxes. Others stack up heavy loads, and then move them around the factory.

Shoulder

Power supply

? What other jobs can you think of that working robots do?

Rotterdam in the Netherlands is the world's busiest sea port. Hundreds of ships come to Rotterdam every day.

Huge robot cranes unload the ships. Robot trucks carry the loads on the dock. No drivers are in the cranes or the trucks. Humans in a large control room instruct the cranes and trucks which job to do next.

GT Record

The T-53 is one of the largest tracked ROVs. It weighs almost 3 tonnes and can be used in search operations after an earthquake.

ONLINE//:

http://www.cat.csiro.au/ict.html
Use this website to find out more about working robots. There are photos to download of an underwater vehicle and mining trucks.

Undersea robots

Some robots work in the ocean. Robotic ROVs can dive down to the ocean floor.

Undersea ROVs shine bright lights and send video images to the scientists working in a ship on the surface. The ROVs use their moveable arms to pick up things.

Other ROVs are shaped like fish, or even **torpedos**. They can travel for months under water. Scientists use them to measure the temperature of the water, and the speed of **ocean currents**.

The Seaglider ROV can stay underwater for months.

GT Record

Many ROVs can travel to a depth of 6,000 metres (m) or more. The ROV Kaiko dived to the deepest part of the ocean, 10,909m, in 1995.

ONLINE//:

http://www.ife.org
The Institute For Exploration uses underwater ROVs to explore under the sea. Search 'Hercules' to find out more about this underwater ROV.

Military robots

Soldiers use small, tough robots to do the most dangerous and difficult jobs.

Bomb-disposal ROVs can find hidden bombs and make them safe. Scout ROVs move into dangerous places where enemy soldiers might be hiding.

GT Top Fact

Military ROVs cannot choose to attack an enemy. They can only attack if they are instructed to by their human controllers.

This is the iRobot PackBot scout. It sends video images to its controller.

Flying robots are known as Unmanned Aerial Vehicles, or UAVs. Military UAVs can fly high above a battlefield.

Scout UAVs send images back to the soldiers on the ground. Hunter UAVs carry explosives. They look for enemies to attack.

ONLINE//:

http://www.irobot.com
iRobot makes many robots and ROVs, including military ones. This website features product details, videos and a 'how they work section'.

How robots work

Robots can't think for themselves. Humans have to plan everything that a robot does. This is called writing a robot's program. The people who write the program are called programmers.

Programmers use computers to plan a robot's task. Once the robot has been programmed it can do a task again and again.

Programmers can 'teach' a robot a new job. The instructions are stored in the robot's 'brain', called a **central processing unit**.

This programmer is connecting a robot to her computer.

ONLINE//:

http://www.abc.net.au/science/slab/robo/default.htm
This website has lots of information about how robots work, robot history, and more real robots (not made-up ones from films).

Robots and ROVs cannot see, hear or feel in the way that humans can. They have sensors and cameras to detect sounds or see objects.

ROVs are guided by their human controllers. Different cameras, including ones that can see in low light, help the controller to move the ROV into the right position.

Mobile robots, such as ASIMO (right), are battery powered. After a few hours, ASIMO needs to **recharge** its batteries. It detects the nearest recharge point and plugs itself in.

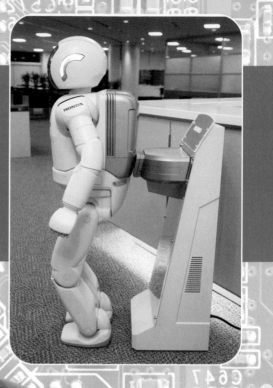

GT Top Fact

Some robot hands have touch sensors. They can hold an egg gently without crushing it. Why do you think this is important?

Fun with robots

Most robots have a job to do. Other robots are built just for fun. People can learn about robots as they build them.

Lego Mindstorms robots look like ordinary Lego models. But you can program these robots, and teach them to work, or even to dance.

GT Top Fact

This humanoid robot is Alpha Rex. You can build other Lego Mindstorms robots from the same kit. These include Spike, the scorpion robot, and Tribot, the three-wheeled robot.

Teams take part in competitions, such as RoboCup and First Lego League, to win robot football games. There are also robot 'rescue' and robot 'dance' competitions.

Older players compete with larger humanoid robots called Nao robots (above). These robots can walk quickly around the playing field.

ONLINE//:

http://www.robocup.org
This is the RoboCup website. It's a great place to find out more about robot football – with downloadable images (click 'Media').

Battling robots

Battle robots are ROVs that are built to fight in competitions. These competitions have included *Robot Wars* and *Battlebots*. The builders give their ROVs weapons to defeat their opponents.

Battle robot weapons include pincers, saws and flippers. The battle robots are usually wide and low. This makes it harder to flip them over.

 Try drawing your own battle robot. What would you call it? What weapons would it have?

Battle robots fight each other in different weight groups. Some are small and light. Other battle robots weigh more than a person.

GT Top Fact

Battle robots are built following important safety rules. They can't use **explosives** or fire, and they can't shoot at the other robots. This would be too dangerous for the audience!

A flipper is a powerful battle robot weapon.

ONLINE//:

www.fightingrobots.co.uk
This is the website of the Fighting Robot Association. Check out the history pages, news updates and links to other robot associations.

Robo Battle Bots

Written by Leon Read   Illustrated by Kevin Hopgood

Battle Axe was amazing – the best robot ever seen. The only problem was that Battle Axe didn't belong to Ikram or his cousin Shahid. Their robot was called Arjan. It had taken a year to build.

BATTLE AXE

- Axe can swing three times a second
- Can self-right if flipped over
- Has motors so powerful the robot can pull a small car

ARJAN

- Flipper can roll over opponents
- Has tough armour
- Can move very quickly

"Why were we picked to fight Battle Axe in the quarter-final?" Shahid complained. "Arjan will be smashed up."

Ikram ignored Shahid. He helped his uncle.

"So, what's your battle plan?" Ikram's uncle asked.
Ikram shrugged. "Just the same. I'll drive and Shahid
activates the flipper."

"I know that. I meant how will you beat Battle Axe?"
his uncle said.

Ikram and Shahid looked at each other. Did he really
think they could?

"We'll avoid the axe," Ikram suggested.

"And run away," Shahid said.

Ikram frowned. "No, we must attack. If we flip
Battle Axe then it can't use the axe."

"Good thinking, Ikram," his uncle said.

Shahid wasn't so sure. "Except if we attack we'll get
smashed up."

Ikram's uncle laughed.

"What's so funny?" they both asked.

"You two! Just remember why you are here."

"To battle!" they said.

"Exactly. But also to work together. It doesn't matter if you lose. You've already won battles to get this far."

Up in the arena control room Ikram and Shahid waited for the countdown. They waved to the crowd.

"Roboteers ready! 3, 2, 1! Activate!"

Battle Axe rushed towards Arjan. Ikram used the controller to turn Arjan away just as the axe smashed into the arena floor.

"Quick!" Shahid screamed.

Arjan span around and raced at Battle Axe, pushing it towards the wall. But Battle Axe was strong, and pushed back. The wheels gripped the floor. The powerful motors whined. Arjan's flipper shot up and caught Battle Axe. But it just span off to the side, and didn't flip over.

Ikram's mouth was dry. His hands were sweaty. There was hardly time to think. Battle Axe swung around and the axe smashed down onto Arjan.

"Move!" Shahid shouted.

Ikram hit reverse, trying to move Arjan away from the axe. But Battle Axe powered forward, smashing its axe down again. Shahid activated the flipper, this time it flipped over Battle Axe!

The crowd cheered loudly. Battle Axe swung its axe and it sprung upright again. The robot powered forward. Its axe slammed down into Arjan. The armour buckled and jammed a wheel. Ikram shifted the contols, but Arjan was stuck! The axe swung down again and again. It dented Arjan's armour but couldn't get through it. Shahid activated the flipper, but Battle Axe was too far away.

Then the buzzer sounded. The battle was over. Arjan had been beaten.

"That was a great battle!" Ikram's uncle said later. He sounded really pleased.

"But we lost," Ikram said.

"That doesn't matter, you were up against the best robot here. Next year we can build an even better robot."

Ikram and Shahid thought about it. "Yes!" Ikram said. "Arjan II."

GT Robot battle words

Activate – to start something, to turn something on

Buckled – badly dented

Self-right – a robot's ability to turn back up the right way after being turned over by another robot's flipper

Robots around the home

There are not many robots working in our homes yet. Scientists once thought that home robots would be easy to make.

Actually, home robots are difficult to make and expensive. There are robot vacuum cleaners (right and below), pool cleaners and lawnmowers.

 What robots would you like in your home?

This is a pool-cleaning robot.

These robots use sensors to work in one area, and can be programmed by humans. They cannot change to do any other job, such as washing the dishes.

GT Top Fact

There is even a robot gutter cleaner, called Looj. It rolls along the gutters of roofs, cleaning out dead leaves.

ONLINE//:

http://www.irobot.com/sp.cfm?pageid=95
Find out more about all the robots on these two pages, plus Scooba the floor-washing robot and Dirt Dog.

Robotic vehicles

Scientists are building robot cars that do not have a driver. This is not as easy as it sounds! Robot vehicles are complicated but could drive safely on roads in the future.

The R-Gator is a military robot vehicle. It can be programmed to follow a team of soldiers with all their gear.

The DARPA Challenge is a competition to see who can build the best robot car. Cars drive in the desert for over 20 kilometres, missing rocks and large holes. In the first DARPA Challenge, none of the cars finished. But in the most recent competition, many cars finished safely.

ONLINE//:

http://www.tartanracing.org
Find out more about Boss, the car shown above, winner of the 2007 DARPA Challenge. The site includes images and news articles.

Robots in space

Space is a dangerous place for humans. But robots can travel into space, and then spend many months or years exploring. They don't need any food, water or air.

Cassini spacecraft

Probe

Some robots are satellites. Their job is to orbit a planet, taking photos and making measurements.

Many other space robots are probes. Some are launched by spacecraft and fall to the surface of a moon or planet. They can use parachutes to land gently. Probes record information and some explore.

GT Top Fact

In 2004, the Cassini spacecraft (left) flew past Titan, one of the moons near Saturn. It released a probe that recorded images as it parachuted to the surface of Titan. Cassini is still exploring Saturn and its moons today.

Other robots will one day work with human astronauts on the space shuttle, or on board the International Space Station.

Robonaut is a humanoid robot. Its job is to help human astronauts when they work outside the shuttle. Its hands can hold tools.

GT Top Fact

It would take 20–24 years to travel to the edge of our solar system. That's too long for human astronauts to be in space, so robots could be sent instead.

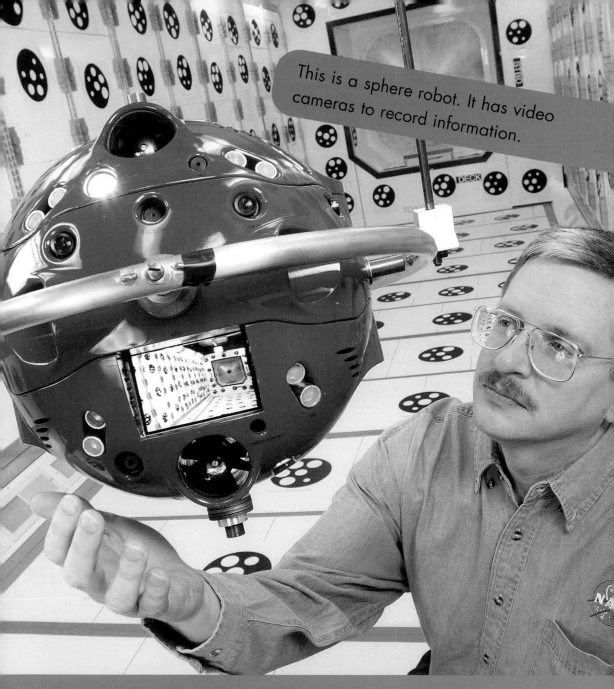

This is a sphere robot. It has video cameras to record information.

Small helper robots will work inside with the astronauts. These robots are round, and will float inside the shuttle. They can move around using tiny fans and send live images directly to the control room on Earth.

ONLINE//:

http://robonaut.jsc.nasa.gov
Robonaut hasn't left Earth yet. See the latest Robonaut news at this site, including videos, and details about Robonaut's parts.

Planet rovers

Rovers are robots designed to move around on the surface of another planet or moon.

The earliest rovers were the Russian Lunokhod rovers, which landed on the Moon in the late 1970s.

In 2004, NASA sent two rovers, Spirit and Opportunity (left), to explore Mars. These two rovers rolled across the surface of Mars for over five years. They found signs of water on Mars.

GT Top Fact

The Mars Science Lab Rover (below) will land on Mars in 2010. It is much larger and faster than Spirit and Opportunity. It will carry out many experiments on the soil and rocks on Mars.

ONLINE//:

http://www.nasa.gov/mission_pages/mer/index.html
On this website you can see photos of the Mars rovers, Spirit and Opportunity, and read the latest mission news.

New robots

Scientists are trying to make new and better robots. Some try to make better humanoid robots. Others are working on robots that don't look human at all.

The most well-known humanoid robot is Honda's ASIMO. It can do many amazing things, including running. Most robots still move around very slowly, but not ASIMO. Perhaps one day there will be many robots like ASIMO working around our homes and in offices.

This robot lift in Germany helps to store and collect cars more quickly than a human-controlled lift.

GT Top Fact

Swarm robots are teams of tiny robots. These ones, created by EPFL, could be used in search-and-rescue missions.

ONLINE//:

http://asimo.honda.com
See ASIMO, the world's most advanced humanoid robot. You can watch ASIMO in action, and download some great images.

Fast facts

The world's largest robot is a huge earthmover. It stands 75m high and weighs 3,500 tonnes. It can shovel up 100–300 tonnes of rock in one scoop.

The cheapest robot ever built cost just £1.15. It was made from an old Sony Walkman.

Sony's AIBO ERS-110 was the fastest-selling robot. 3,000 were sold in 20 minutes!

The world's first factory robot worked in the General Motors car factory, USA, in 1961.

The world's smallest robots are so tiny 200 could fit across a plain M&M sweet. They could be used to check electrical equipment.

The world's fastest humanoid robot is made by Hitachi. It's called the Emiew and travels at 6**kph** (but it does have wheels).

Answers

These are suggestions to questions in this book. You may find that you have other answers. Talk about them with your friends. They may have other answers too.

Pages 7, 30: The answers to these questions will depend on your own choices.

Page 9: There are many jobs that working robots do including lifting heavy things, moving stuff, digging rock, cutting metal, etc. These are often jobs that can be done more quickly by a robot, or that are dangerous.

Page 19: It might be important for robots to pick things up gently without crushing them. This could be useful for a rescue robot holding a person. Holding objects gently is one of the most difficult things for robots to do. Their hands and arms have sensors that detect how much **pressure** is needed to hold an object safely.

Page 22: You could think of tough-sounding names, such as Iron Fist, Mega Axe or Blade. Some robot names are funny, such as Fluffy and Pussycat. Don't forget to follow the safety rules for weapons. Flippers are quick, axes and saws cut armour, and pincers can crush.

More websites

Webpage from Aldebaran Robotics, the company that makes Nao robots for the RoboCup, featuring short videos:

http://www.aldebaran-robotics.com/eng/Movieclip.php

Home of the British Automation and Robot Association. This website has up-to-date robot news and downloadable documents and videos:

http://www.bara.org.uk

Lots of videos of working factory robots:

http://www.robots.com/movies.php

This website features battle robots made with Lego Mindstorms parts. It includes photos and battle videos:

http://www.battlebricks.com

Robot gateway on The Tech website, featuring a history of robots and a chance to control an ROV online:

http://www.thetech.org/robotics

Website of the Heart Robot – an amazing, expressive robot. Also features other robot designs, plus videos:

http://www.heartrobot.org.uk

Website of Wowwee, makers of the award-winning Robosapien humanoid robot. Includes videos, adverts, and photos of their robot models:

www.wowwee.com

Robot exhibition webpage of MIT (Massachusetts Institute of Technology):

http://web.mit.edu/museum/exhibitions/robots.html

Glossary

Central processing unit – an electronic circuit, also called a microprocessor, which forms a computer's 'brain'.

Explosive – something that can explode (burst with a loud bang). Fireworks are explosives.

GPS – (global positioning system) a satellite system that allows people or robots to find their position anywhere on Earth.

IR sensor – (infrared sensor) a sensor that uses a form of red light which cannot be seen by people. IR sensors can be used to detect movement and distance.

Kph – short for kilometres per hour, a measurement of distance travelled and the time taken.

Ocean currents – the flow and movement of large amounts of water in the ocean.

Pressure – the name of the force that takes place when one thing squeezes or squashes another thing. Hands and fingers apply pressure to an object when they pick it up.

Probe – (space probe) a space vehicle used by scientists to record information, such as temperatures, about other planets.

Recharge – to store up electricity in an electronic object. Rechargable batteries store the electrcity.

Remotely – from a distance. A Remotely Operated Vehicle (ROV) can be controlled from anywhere within a certain control range – and usually from a safe distance!

Torpedo – a tube-shaped missile launched underwater, usually by a submarine.

Welder – a tool used to join pieces of metal together. A car welder uses heat and pressure to join door hinges to a car body.

Index

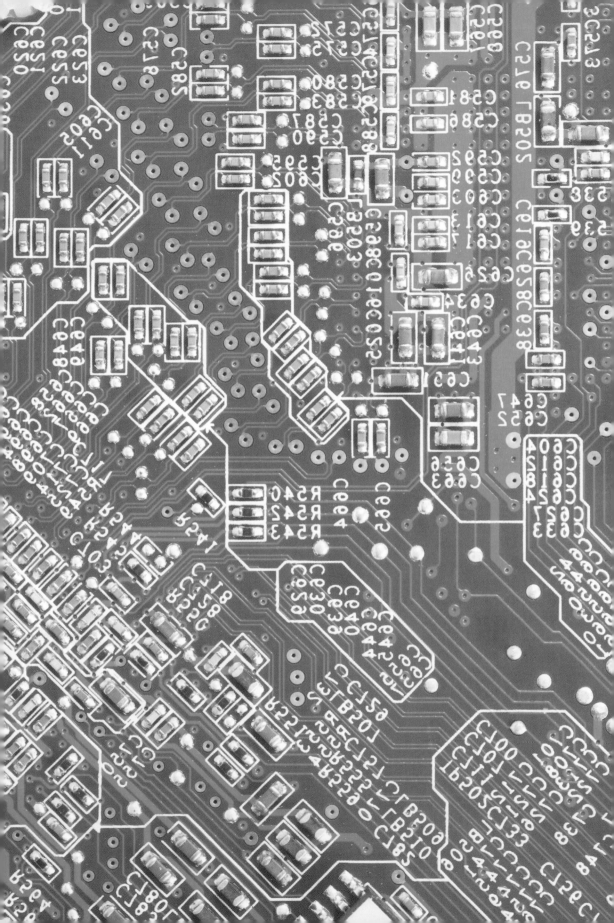

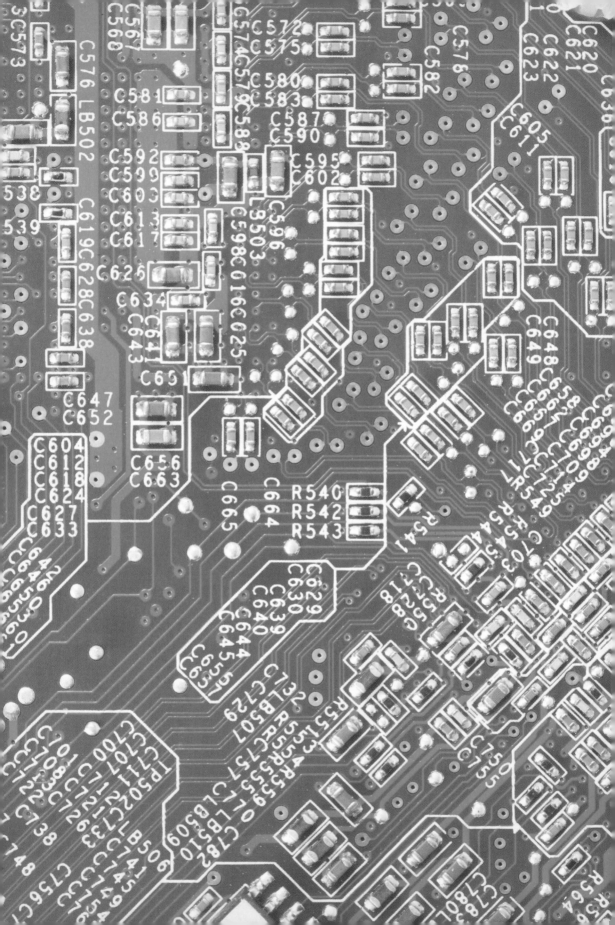